THE SPREAD OF HATE AND EXTREMISM

Robert M. Henderson

ReferencePoint Press®

San Diego, CA

ReferencePoint Press®

About the Author

Robert M. Henderson has worked as an editor and copywriter for more than thirty years. He is the author of National Geographic's *World Regions: West Asia*. He currently lives in Vermont.

For more information, contact:
ReferencePoint Press, Inc.
PO Box 27779
San Diego, CA 92198
www.ReferencePointPress.com

Picture Credits:
Cover: Kim Kelley-Wagner/Shutterstock.com

6: Carol Guzy/ZUMA Press/Newscom
11: Associated Press
15: Everett Collection/Bridgeman Images
18: Associated Press
21: littleny/iStock
24: Everett Collection/Shutterstock.com
29: Shutterstock.com
33: Vasin Lee/Shutterstock.com
37: Daniel Krason/Shutterstock.com
40: Jazzmany/Shutterstock.com
47: Jeff Wheeler/ZUMA Press/Newscom
49: John Rudoff/Polaris/Newscom
53: iStock
55: Shutterstock.com
57: a katz/Shutterstock.com
63: Karen Focht/ZUMA Press/Newscom

LIBRARY OF CONGRESS CATALOGING-IN-PUBLICATION DATA

Names: Henderson, Robert M., author.
Title: The spread of hate and extremism / Robert M. Henderson.
Description: San Diego : ReferencePoint Press, 2020. | Includes
   bibliographical references and index.
Identifiers: LCCN 2020000102 (print) | LCCN 2020000103 (ebook) | ISBN
   9781682829332 (library binding) | ISBN 9781682829349 (ebook)
Subjects: LCSH: Hate crimes--United States--Juvenile literature. | Hate
   crimes--Law and legislation--United States--Juvenile literature.
Classification: LCC HV6773.52 .H46 2020 (print) | LCC HV6773.52 (ebook) |
   DDC 364.150973--dc23
LC record available at https://lccn.loc.gov/2020000102
LC ebook record available at https://lccn.loc.gov/2020000103

NOV - 1 2020

CONTENTS

INTRODUCTION

A Growing Threat

On a sunny Saturday morning in August 2019, a young white man walked into a Walmart in El Paso, Texas, and opened fire with a semiautomatic rifle, killing twenty-two people and injuring twenty-four others. Shortly before the shooting, the suspect had posted a four-page manifesto filled with white nationalist and anti-immigrant rhetoric on an anonymous internet message board. The document warned of an impending attack. When the police arrested the suspect, he told them that he was specifically targeting Mexicans.

El Paso, Texas, stands on the Rio Grande, a natural border between the United States and Mexico. Its population is 80 percent Hispanic. "What was most shocking to me is not that it was a mass shooting but the motive, the fact that he specifically targeted Mexican-Americans and Hispanics," said librarian Gilda Baeza Ortega. "He came here for us."[1]

The El Paso massacre was the deadliest attack against Latinos in modern American history. It came just ten months after another mass shooting, this time targeting Jews in Pittsburgh, Pennsylvania. On October 27, 2018, a gunman with an assault rifle and three semiautomatic pistols walked into the Tree of Life synagogue during the Saturday morning Shabbat services.

Shouting "All Jews must die!,"[2] he opened fire, killing eleven people and injuring seven more. It was the deadliest attack on the Jewish community in US history.

These horrific shootings are not isolated incidents but are part of a growing trend of hate and extremism in the United States. "There are more hate groups, more hate crimes, and more domestic terrorism," says Heidi Beirich of the Southern Poverty Law Center (SPLC). "It is a troubling set of circumstances."[3]

The Rise of Hate Groups in America

According to a 2018 report by the SPLC, a record-high 1,020 hate groups are operating in the United States. The SPLC, which monitors extremism and hate groups, reports that 2018 was the fourth year in a row that the number of hate groups in the United States had risen.

The SPLC notes that not all hate groups are the same, but they share one defining characteristic: they vilify "others because of their race, religion, ethnicity, sexual orientation, or gender identity—prejudices that strike at the heart of our democratic values and fracture society along its most fragile fault lines."[4]

> "What was most shocking to me is not that it was a mass shooting but the motive, the fact that he specifically targeted Mexican-Americans and Hispanics. He came here for us."[1]
>
> —Gilda Baeza Ortega, El Paso librarian

There are many categories of hate groups, including white nationalist, racist skinhead, Ku Klux Klan, neo-Nazi, black nationalist, neo-Confederate, Christian Identity, anti-Muslim, anti-immigrant, and anti-LGBTQ. An organization does not have to actively engage in violent activity to be listed as a hate group. It can also qualify if the group's ideology can inspire and motivate *others* to do violence.

Many, but not all, hate groups are unified by one overriding ideology—white supremacy. This is the idea that white people and their culture are superior to other peoples and cultures and should therefore dominate. As the United States becomes more ethnically

A family visits the memorial site where a white man walked into a Walmart in El Paso, Texas, in August 2019 and opened fire with a rifle, killing twenty-two people. The suspect told police that he was specifically targeting Mexicans.

diverse, many white supremacists fear that, unless immediate action is taken, nonwhites will eventually take over the country.

The El Paso and Pittsburgh shooters were both motivated by white supremacist ideology. In his manifesto, the El Paso shooter called his attack "a response to the Hispanic invasion of Texas."[5] And the Pittsburgh shooter told police, "They're committing genocide to my people. . . . I just want to kill Jews."[6]

Startling Statistics

The El Paso and Pittsburgh shooters were both homegrown, born and raised in the United States. Until recently, most Americans believed that foreign terrorists were the most likely to commit such acts of mass murder. After all, since the September 11, 2001, terrorist attacks on the United States, government officials have focused almost exclusively on foreign individuals and groups as potential threats. But they ignored a threat closer to home. Since 9/11 more lives have been lost due to domestic terrorist attacks—such as the El Paso and Pittsburgh shootings—than to foreign terrorists. In fact, no foreign terrorist organization has conducted a deadly attack inside the United States since 9/11. And dramatic shootings like those in El Paso and Pittsburgh tend to overshadow the increasing number of incidents involving harassment and nondeadly violence against blacks, Jews, Muslims, Hispanics, and other groups. Overall, statistics released by the FBI show that violent personal attacks motivated by bias or prejudice reached a sixteen-year high in 2018.

The spread of hate and extremism is not confined to the United States. Mass shootings motivated by white supremacism have occurred in Norway, New Zealand, and other countries around the world. White supremacism was once thought to exist only on the margins of society, but many experts now believe it is infiltrating the mainstream. Erroll Southers, a professor of national and homeland security at the University of Southern California in Los Angeles, says, "I don't think it's (white supremacy) . . . a fringe movement, it is certainly coming of age. It is being globalized at a very rapid pace."[7]

> "I don't think it's (white supremacy) . . . a fringe movement, it is certainly coming of age. It is being globalized at a very rapid pace."[7]
>
> —Erroll Southers, professor of national and homeland security at the University of Southern California

A Danger to Democracy

Hate, and the violence it inspires, does not just affect the immediate victims—it poses a threat to the very foundations of democracy. Hate and extremism create fear and terror, which is often magnified by politicians and the media. Daniel L. Byman, a Senior Fellow at the Center for Middle East Policy, warns, "The fear terrorism generates can distort public debates, discredit moderates, empower political extremes, and polarize societies."[8]

Fear and polarization feed off each other, creating an unhealthy environment for democracies to function in. Not surprisingly, the growing number of hate groups and hate crimes in recent years coincides with an increased sense of polarization in the United

States. According to the Pew Research Center, Democrats and Republicans in the United States increasingly see each other as a threat to the nation's well-being. This results in government inaction, since both parties are loath to compromise on any issue. Meanwhile, 85 percent of Americans say that political debate in the country has become more negative and less respectful, while 76 percent say it has become less fact based.

The poisonous atmosphere created by polarization can encourage people to lie and deceive in order to defeat their perceived enemies. Polarization also affects the dynamics *within* a group, since people feel more pressure to think and act in ways that conform to the group's identity. This makes dissent and diversity less likely, since people fear giving offense.

When dissent, compromise, and honesty are stifled, even mature democracies like those in the United States and Europe struggle to function. This allows extremist political movements that feed on polarization to grow in power. The result is that societies all over the world, after decades of relative stability, are now racked with deep divisions.

CHAPTER ONE

The Changing Face of Hate

If you asked someone to name one white supremacist hate group, they would most likely answer the Ku Klux Klan (KKK). The KKK is the most notorious racist group in US history. Klan members' terrifying white hoods and robes and the burning crosses they place in front of people's homes are icons of hatred. While most of today's white supremacists do not wear costumes or burn crosses, they are still motivated by the same basic ideology that motivates the KKK—the idea that whites are superior to other races and should dominate people of other backgrounds.

The KKK was born after the Civil War, in the smoking rubble of the Confederacy. Its founding members— six former Confederate soldiers from Tennessee—saw themselves as representing white people in the South who had lost power. They strongly resented slaves being given their freedom and having more rights. Early KKK meetings soon turned more sinister as members discussed ways to intimidate former slaves in order to regain some of the power white southerners had lost in the Civil War. Eventually, the KKK evolved into a large terrorist organization covering multiple states. Klan members, dressed in white robes and pointed hoods, would ride their horses at night and terrorize any black people they could find. Blacks were often whipped, beaten, and hung from trees, or "lynched."

Attempting to convince Congress that the South had not learned its lesson in the Civil War, President Ulysses S. Grant spelled out the aim of the KKK: "By force and terror . . . to deprive colored citizens of the right to bear arms and of the right of a free ballot, to suppress the schools in which colored children were taught, and to reduce the colored people to a condition closely allied to that of slavery."[9] In 1871 the government passed the Ku Klux Klan Act, which authorized the president to use all the power at his disposal for the purpose of destroying the KKK. This proved successful, and the KKK was temporarily put out of business.

Jim Crow Laws

Despite being disbanded, the aim of the KKK was achieved anyway, thanks to the US government. In the late 1800s a series of laws were enacted that enforced racial segregation throughout the South. These came to be called Jim Crow laws in reference to a pejorative name for a black person. In 1896 the Supreme Court upheld these laws in the case of *Plessy v. Ferguson*, in which the court laid out its "separate but equal" doctrine for African Americans. This doctrine stated that racially segregating blacks did not violate the Fourteenth Amendment, which guarantees equal protection to all people.

Under Jim Crow laws, blacks were segregated from whites in public parks, at beaches, on buses, and in schools. Blacks had to use separate drinking fountains, restrooms, and restaurants. The facilities reserved for blacks were vastly inferior to those used by whites, if they even existed at all.

The KKK itself lay largely dormant until 1915, when the silent film *The Birth of a Nation* by D.W. Griffith helped spark its rebirth. The film quotes a line from a book written by a renowned historian: "At last there had sprung into existence a great Ku Klux Klan, a veritable empire of the South, to protect the Southern country."[10] The renowned historian was US president Woodrow

Wilson, the former president of Princeton University. By the 1920s a revived KKK claimed 4 million to 5 million members, representing about 15 percent of the total population in the United States.

The KKK lost popularity during World War II, when the United States unified to defeat Adolf Hitler and the Nazis. It surged again during the civil rights era in the 1950s and 1960s, when Jim Crow laws were being challenged. Bus boycotts, restaurant lunch counter sit-ins, and other acts of civil disobedience fueled the civil rights movement, which ultimately led to the total abolishment of Jim Crow laws by 1965.

Throughout most of its history, the KKK has worked to support and enforce Jim Crow laws, which institutionalized educational, social, and economic disadvantages for people of color in the South. With the end of the Jim Crow laws, the KKK seemed to lose its purpose.

New Objectives

Today's KKK has only a few thousand members. According to the SPLC, "The KKK has not been able to appeal to younger racists, with its antiquated traditions, odd dress and lack of

Ku Klux Klan members in Florida watch as a large cross burns in 1939. Today, white supremacists do not usually wear costumes or burn crosses, but they are still motivated by the same basic ideology as the KKK.

digital savvy."[11] In addition, younger racists, knowing that today's America is far less amenable to white supremacists than it was during the days of Jim Crow, try to distance themselves from openly racist hate groups like the KKK.

In fact, it is not unusual to hear today's racists echo what one leading white supremacist had to say in a 2018 interview: "I'm not a white supremacist. I'm not even a white nationalist. I consider myself a civil and human rights advocate focusing on the underrepresented Caucasian demographic."[12]

Another difference between yesterday's KKK and today's racist hate groups are their objectives. The KKK was trying to preserve segregationist Jim Crow laws. "Today, white supremacists and certainly white nationalists want to overthrow the system they live under," says Leonard Zeskind, a founder of the Institute for Research & Education on Human Rights. "They do not want to preserve it. They want to destroy it."[13]

Many of today's hate groups fantasize about creating a state that only white people can live in. Often referred to as the Northwest Territorial Imperative, this state would stretch from Montana to Oregon and Washington State. In this state, says Heidi Beirich, director of the SPLC's Intelligence Project,

all civil rights for nonwhites would be removed. All political power would be in the hands of white people, in particular white men because this movement is an extremely male and, many would say, toxically masculine movement. They also have pretty retrograde views about what women should be doing. If anything, their vision of America's future looks a lot like the 1600s or perhaps earlier.[14]

The Great Replacement Theory

While the KKK sought to maintain its power over nonwhites, today's racist groups often project a sense of white victimhood. "There is a sense that whites are under siege and being deliberately dispossessed by hostile elites who wish to usher in a new multicultural order,"[15] says George Hawley, a political scientist at the University of Alabama.

The idea that whites are under siege is often referred to as the "great replacement" conspiracy theory, which is very similar to

Black Nationalism

Not all hate groups are grounded in white supremacist ideology. As the number of white hate groups has grown, so has the number of radical black nationalist groups that consistently bash Jews, white people, the police, and gays and transgendered people. Many black nationalists want to form separate institutions for African Americans—or even a separate nation.

One of the wealthiest and most well known black nationalist groups is the Nation of Islam, founded in Detroit, Michigan, in 1930. The Nation of Islam is listed as a hate group by the SPLC. Its current leader, Louis Farrakhan, often accuses President Donald Trump of "planning genocide" against African Americans. He has also said that "powerful Jews are my enemy" and claimed that "the Jews were responsible for all of this filth and degenerate behavior that Hollywood is putting out turning men into women and women into men." In 2017 Farrakhan tweeted, "Black People: We should be more convinced that it is time for us to separate and build a nation of our own." Many prominent members of the alt-right movement expressed their support for Farrakhan's statement.

Black nationalist groups should not be confused with organizations such as Black Lives Matter that promote social justice and the dismantling of institutional racism in America. And black nationalist groups are not nearly as violent as many white supremacist groups. Finally, unlike white hate groups, black nationalist groups have failed to find a place in mainstream politics.

Quoted in Anti-Defamation League, "Farrakhan: In His Own Words," 2013. www.adl.org.
Quoted in Southern Poverty Law Center, "Nation of Islam." www.splcenter.org.

"white genocide" or "white replacement" theories. Taken together, these conspiracy theories form the basis of most far-right ideologies and are the main catalysts for far-right violence and mass attacks.

The El Paso and Pittsburgh shooters were both obsessed with the great replacement and white genocide theories. In his manifesto, the El Paso shooter writes, "I am simply defending my country from cultural and ethnic replacement brought on by an invasion."[16] Meanwhile, the Pittsburgh shooter told police that Jews were perpetrating genocide against his people.

Many of today's racists assert that "whiteness" is just another form of diversity that is in danger of becoming extinct. White people and culture must be protected, they say, just like other races. This allows white nationalists to avoid seeming racist—while still promoting racist views. Thomas Chatterton Williams, a journalist and author who has written extensively about race, says using this kind of language "is simply rhetorically pragmatic because the purpose is to popularize a viewpoint and attract as many sympathetic onlookers as possible. Today, open racism will only ever be a truly marginal position. It repels too many who could potentially otherwise be reached."[17]

> "Today, open racism will only ever be a truly marginal position. It repels too many who could potentially otherwise be reached."[17]
>
> —Thomas Chatterton Williams, author of *Self-Portrait in Black and White*

Rebranding Hate and Extremism

Because open racism is not tolerated by today's society, robes, hoods, and Nazi uniforms have mostly disappeared as symbols of white supremacy. Instead, members of these groups dress like everyone else. "We need to be extremely conscious of what we look like, and how we present ourselves," wrote a prominent American neo-Nazi before a big 2017 rally. "That matters more than our ideas. If that is sad to you, I'm sorry, but that is just human nature. If people see a bunch of mismatched overweight slobs, they are not going to care what they are saying."[18]

Today's white supremacists not only dress differently from their forebears, they also use different words to describe themselves and their views. "I don't use the term white nationalist to describe myself," says leading white supremacist Richard Spencer. "I like the term Alt-Right. It has an openness to it. And immediately un-derstandable. We're coming from a new perspective."[19]

Spencer began using the name Alternative Right for an online publication he began in 2010. The term *alt-right* is now commonly used in mainstream media to describe people on the extreme right who reject modern conservatism for not advocating strongly enough for the interests of white people. But the term *alt-right* is simply a rebranding, according to Oren Segal, director of the Anti-Defamation League's (ADL) Center on Extremism—"a new name for this old hatred."[20]

The alt-right is an extremely loose movement with no formal organization or membership. Most of the people who identify with it are anonymous and online. Historian Matthew N. Lyons has de-fined the alt-right as a "far-right movement that shares a contempt for both liberal multiculturalism and mainstream conservatism; a

An African American man stands at a segregated bus stop in 1940. Under Jim Crow laws, blacks were segregated from whites in schools as well as other public areas and facilities.

COLORED WAITING ROOM

PRIVATE PROPERTY
NO PARKING
Driving through or Turning Around

belief that some people are inherently superior to others; a strong Internet presence and embrace of specific elements of online culture; and a self-presentation as being new, hip, and irreverent."[21]

The alt-right is notable for its success in appealing to young people using online forums, videos, and humorous memes.

Symbols of Hate

The Anti-Defamation League (ADL) has put together a database of nearly two hundred symbols associated with hate groups. These symbols continue to evolve, and in 2019 the ADL added thirty-six new entries to its database, which already includes the swastika, KKK costumes, burning crosses, and many other symbols of racism and anti-Semitism. Newer entries include the following:

The OK hand gesture—The OK sign has been used in memes and other images promoting hate. The Australian suspected of killing fifty-one people at mosques in New Zealand flashed the OK sign in court after his arrest.

Moon Man—This character was featured in old McDonald's commercials but has since been appropriated by the alt-right, which has turned it into a racist hip-hop performer.

The Bowl Cut—This hairstyle was worn by the white supremacist who fatally shot nine black churchgoers in Charleston, South Carolina, in 2015.

Pepe the Frog—The green cartoon frog with big eyes was hijacked by the alt-right, which attached symbols of racism and anti-Semitism to it.

The Hate on Display database was launched by the ADL in 2000 to help police officers, school officials, and others recognize signs of hate and extremism. According to ADL chief executive officer Jonathan Greenblatt, "Even as extremists continue to use symbols that may be years or decades old, they regularly create new symbols, memes, and slogans to express their hateful sentiments."

Quoted in Associated Press, "'OK' Hand Gesture, 'Bowlcut' Added to Hate Symbols Database," NBC News, September 26, 2019. www.nbcnews.com.

Those who feel alienated or misunderstood can easily use their smartphones to connect with young alt-right influencers who seem edgy and cool. Alt-righters avoid using terms like race and white identity and instead present themselves as people who enjoy questioning authority, which often appeals to naturally rebellious teenagers.

Unite the Right Rally

In 2017 the alt-right attempted to move from an online-based to a street-based movement with the Unite the Right rally in Charlottesville, Virginia. Organizers Richard Spencer and Jason Kessler wanted to unite all the strands of the white nationalist movement. They chose as their focal point the proposed removal of the statue of Confederate general Robert E. Lee from Charlottesville's Lee Park.

Many government officials want to remove Confederate statues and monuments from public areas. Most of these memorials were erected during the Jim Crow era, and many people see them not so much as memorials but as a means of intimidating blacks and reaffirming white supremacy.

The Unite the Right rally featured various alt-right, white supremacist, neo-Nazi, neo-Confederate, neofascist, white nationalist, and other far-right groups. On the evening of August 11, the event turned violent when protesters fought with counterprotesters, injuring dozens. On the morning of August 12, the governor of Virginia declared a state of emergency and an unlawful assembly when physical altercations between protesters began to escalate. At 1:45 p.m. a white supremacist used his car as a weapon when he drove into a large group of counterprotesters, killing thirty-two-year-old Heather Heyer and injuring nineteen other people. The perpetrator is currently serving life imprisonment for his actions.

President Donald Trump's remarks on Charlottesville were highly controversial. Trump did not explicitly denounce the right-wing marchers or the act that led to one woman's death. Rather, he criticized "hatred, bigotry, and violence on many sides" and referred to "very fine people on both sides."[22]

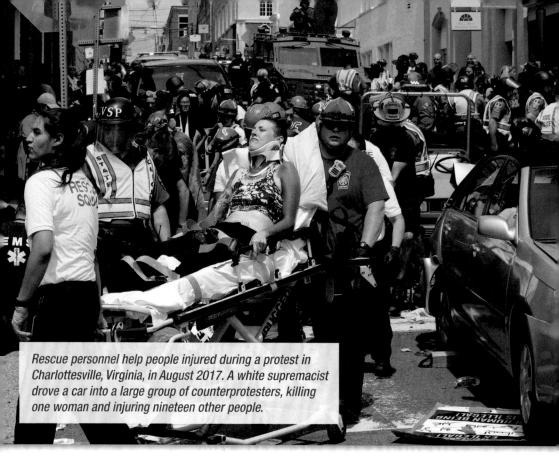

Rescue personnel help people injured during a protest in Charlottesville, Virginia, in August 2017. A white supremacist drove a car into a large group of counterprotesters, killing one woman and injuring nineteen other people.

Reaction to Trump's comments were mixed. More than sixty members of Congress, both Democrats and Republicans, condemned Trump's remarks. "It is not too much to ask to have a president who explicitly condemns Nazis,"[23] says Democratic senator Brian Schatz of Hawaii.

However, one neo-Nazi website praised the president's comments. "He didn't attack us. He just said the nation should come together. Nothing specific against us," wrote the website's founder. "No condemnation at all. When asked to condemn, he just walked out of the room. Really, really good. God bless him."[24]

Many alt-righters saw the Unite the Right rally as a failure. The violence and murder of a counterprotester triggered a backlash against white supremacist groups. Many of the rally's participants were identified by photographs and publicly shamed. Their financial and social media accounts were shut down. Some lost their jobs.

In the aftermath of Charlottesville, many white supremacist leaders started telling their followers to avoid public confrontations while continuing to spread their ideas in a more subtle manner—at small local groups, at underground music venues, and online. By persistently using these tactics, extremists hope to avoid making headlines while gathering more followers. Their goal remains the same—to strategically infiltrate the mainstream, especially in the realm of politics.

Politics of Hate

New research shows that this approach may be working. According to a study conducted by political scientist George Hawley, over 5 percent of white people in America share the alt-right's position that white interests should be promoted. This amounts to about 11 million Americans—and a potentially large bloc of voters. Recognizing this, a record number of far-right extremists ran for state and national office in 2018, according to the ADL.

There is nothing new about extremists being involved in politics, but historically the major political parties have kept these candidates at arm's length. While the Republican Party has publicly denounced most of its extreme candidates, the ADL asserts that some still campaign as Republicans These candidates have possibly been emboldened by the numerous studies which show that Trump's election victory was at least partly driven by racial resentment among white voters.

While Trump has repeatedly condemned white supremacism and far-right ideology, most extremist leaders fully support his presidency. As former KKK grand wizard David Duke told crowds in Charlottesville just prior to the violence, "We are determined to take our country back. We are going to fulfill the promises of Donald Trump. That's what we believed in. That's why we voted for Donald Trump, because he said he's going to take our country back."[25]

CHAPTER TWO

Ripe Conditions for Hate

Hate and extremism thrive under certain political and socioeconomic conditions. The aftermath of the Civil War, for example, diminished the power of whites in the South while increasing the status of blacks. White southerners were angry, afraid of retaliation from former slaves, and distrustful of the US government. These conditions created a perfect environment for the birth and growth of virulent hate groups like the KKK. As Brian Levin, director of the Center for the Study of Hate and Extremism at California State University, San Bernardino, says, "Times of change, fear and conflict offer extremists and conspiracists a chance to present themselves as an alternative to increasingly distrusted traditional mainstream choices."[26] While the conditions today are very different than they were after the Civil War, there are some similarities that are helping fuel the current rise in hate and extremism.

Immigration and Demographics

Immigration and changing demographics are reshaping many countries around the world, including the United States. The US Census Bureau projects that whites will become a minority in the United States by 2045. At that time, no single group will be a majority—the country will consist of a variety of ethnic and racial groups.

This prediction has created an anxiety among some white people who fear a loss of power and identity, resulting in a backlash against people of color, including blacks, Hispanics, Asians, and especially immigrants.

According to national surveys, immigration has replaced terrorism as a top concern in the United States. Some Americans believe that immigrants take away jobs from native workers, depress wages, increase crime, and drain the country's resources. However, the evidence does not support these beliefs. This leads some experts to consider other factors. "It is time to admit an uncomfortable truth," writes Ana Rodriguez, director of the SMU Cox Latino Leadership Initiative. "Economic concerns do not drive fear of immigration. The changing face of America's demographics drive that fear."[27]

> "It is time to admit an uncomfortable truth. Economic concerns do not drive fear of immigration. The changing face of America's demographics drive that fear."[27]
>
> —Ana Rodriguez, director of the SMU Cox Latino Leadership Initiative

People wait to cross the street at a busy intersection in New York City. Immigration and changing demographics are reshaping many countries around the world, including the United States.

Studies have shown that people in countries all over the world vastly exaggerate the size of their immigrant populations. They also overestimate immigrants' poverty levels and their dependence on welfare. About one in seven Americans believes that the average immigrant gets double the amount of government aid compared to native residents. In France a quarter of the population believes this. But in no country is this true. "People who are against immigration generate a sense of crisis," says economist Alberto Alesina. "They create a sense that 'This is a huge problem; we need a wall.'"[28]

Some people on the far right see immigration and changing demographics as a large-scale threat to the very existence of white

Incels

On April 23, 2018, a rented van driven by a young man jumped the curb on a busy street in Toronto, Canada, and intentionally hit dozens of pedestrians, killing ten and injuring fifteen. Most of the victims were women. Just before the attack, the driver had posted a hostile message toward women on Facebook. "The Incel Rebellion has already begun!" the posting read. "We will overthrow all the Chads and Stacys!"

Incels are members of an online community who cannot find a sexual or romantic partner despite wanting one. Incels—short for "involuntarily celibates"—are misogynists (people who hate women). Some incels advocate rape and other forms of violence against women. The van driver's vow to "overthrow all the Chads and Stacys" uses coded language familiar to incels. "Chads" are men who are successful with women, while "Stacys" are women who reject incels. The "Incel Rebellion" would overthrow what incels view as the oppressive feminism of society.

According to the SPLC, incels are a relatively new, and especially virulent, form of male supremacy. "Incel forums tend to have more violent rhetoric than I'm used to seeing on even white supremacist sites," says Keegan Hankes, a senior research analyst at the SPLC.

Quoted in Niraj Chokshi, "What Is an Incel? A Term Used by the Toronto Van Attack Suspect, Explained," *New York Times*, April 24, 2018. www.nytimes.com.

Quoted in Jesselyn Cook, "A Toxic 'Brotherhood': Inside Incels' Dark Online World," HuffPost, July 27, 2018. www.huffpost.com.

people. A popular white supremacist slogan known as the "14 words" says, "We must secure the existence of our people and a future for white children."[29] The idea that the white race is facing extinction is a key concept for many hate groups. In fact, the most popular hashtag that white supremacists use on Twitter is "white genocide." While it is true that immigration and changing demographics will create more diverse societies in many countries, the idea of white genocide is pure fantasy. According to Monica Duffy Toft, a leading scholar on ethnic and religious violence, the recent rise in white nationalism is "due to decades of demographic decline for white Americans combined with a serious decline in public education standards that leads to unwarranted nostalgia and openness to conspiracy theories."[30]

The Election of Barack Obama

On November 4, 2008, an event occurred that crystallized the fear that some white people felt about losing power and status—the election of Barack Obama, the nation's first African American president. For millions of Americans, Obama delivered a message of hope. For white supremacists, he lit a powder keg. "Obama is a visual aid for white Americans who just don't get it yet that we have lost control of our country,"[31] former KKK leader David Duke wrote shortly before Obama was elected president.

In the immediate aftermath of Obama's election, more than two hundred hate-related incidents were reported—a record in modern presidential elections. Obama's election became a potent new recruiting tool for white supremacists, and hate groups such as the KKK and the Council of Conservative Citizens experienced a flood of interest from possible new members. Levin says, "They recognize Obama as a tipping point, the perfect storm in the narrative of the hate world—the apocalypse that they've been moaning about has come true."[32]

> "They recognize Obama as a tipping point, the perfect storm in the narrative of the hate world—the apocalypse that they've been moaning about has come true."[32]
>
> —Brian Levin, director of the Center for the Study of Hate and Extremism at California State University, San Bernardino

Some whites promoted a theory that alleged Obama was not born in the United States and was therefore ineligible to become president. According to the theory, Obama's birth certificate had been forged and he was really born in Kenya, not Hawaii. At the time, one in four Americans (and more than half of all Republicans) believed in this theory, indicating a broad willingness to view Obama's presidency as illegitimate. Those who promoted this theory were called "birthers." Foremost among them was Donald Trump, who would later succeed Obama as president.

Nowhere was white antipathy to Barack Obama stronger than in the Deep South, where he received only 16 percent of white votes in 2008 compared with 90 percent of black votes. The election revealed a gaping racial divide in the Deep South. Black voters felt Obama would represent their views and interests; white voters had the opposite perspective.

On November 4, 2008, Barack Obama became the first African American president of the United States. Obama's election became a potent new recruiting tool for white supremacists and hate groups.

Women's Rights

Over the past fifty years, women have made great strides toward equality, both in the workplace and in politics. As of 2020 a record number of women were serving in Congress, and women continue to speak out against sexual violence, barriers to top positions in business, the pay gap between men and women, and other forms of inequality and oppression.

For some men, however, these feminist gains represent a threat. They believe women are biologically and intellectually inferior to men and that women should play a subservient role in society. This idea is called male supremacy, and those who adhere to its beliefs often participate in loosely organized online communities that are known for directing hate, anger, and violence toward women. As one leading male supremacist writes, "As men, it is our responsibility to . . . lead [women] into their natural roles as wives and mothers. . . . We reward [women] for their willingness to please us and make us happy, and in doing so make themselves happy. No amount of phony education or career 'success' will scratch that deep itch in a girl's soul: the desire to serve a man."[33]

For the first time, the SPLC categorized male supremacy as an explicit hate ideology in 2018. SPLC analyst Keegan Hankes calls male supremacy a "fundamental foundation" of many far-right groups. "The vilification of women by these groups makes them no different than other hate groups that malign an entire class of people,"[34] he says.

According to the SPLC, male supremacist ideology represents all women as "genetically inferior, manipulative, and stupid"[35] beings who exist primarily for sex. Male supremacists blame a large feminist conspiracy for all the problems faced by (mostly white) men today. Not all male supremacists are racist, says the SPLC, and not every racist is a male supremacist, but a deep-seated hatred of women is shared by many of those on the far right.

LGBTQ Rights

The LGBTQ community is another group that has made tremendous progress recently. Gay people are more visible and accepted by society than ever before. In 1988 only 11.6 percent of respondents to a survey thought that same-sex couples should have the right to marry. Today that number is 68 percent, and in 2015 the Supreme Court legalized same-sex marriage throughout the United States. Stanford sociologist Michael Rosenfeld says, "There's more and more rapid change in attitudes towards gay rights in the past 30 years in the United States than there ever has been in recorded attitudes in the United States on any issue."[36]

The flip side of society's increasing acceptance of the LGBTQ community is that some people who strongly oppose it have become more radical. Many anti-LGBTQ hate groups link homosexuality to pedophilia and believe in a conspiracy called the "homosexual agenda," which seeks to undermine Christianity and destroy society. These groups feel that "the way they see the world is threatened, which motivates them to strike out in some way, and for some people, that way could be in violent attacks,"[37] says Gregory M. Herek, a psychology professor at the University of California, Davis, who is an expert on anti-gay violence.

The number of hate crimes stemming from anti-LGBTQ bias has increased five years in a row. They make up nearly 19 percent of the total number of hate crime incidents reported in 2018, according to the FBI's Hate Crime Statistics report. But many believe the statistics vastly underestimate the severity of the problem. According to the Bureau of Justice Statistics, most hate crimes against the LGBTQ community are not reported to the police. "If someone comes forward to report a hate crime, they could also be officially outing themselves as LGBTQ," says Robin Maril, Human Rights Campaign associate legal director. "In a smaller or rural community, that outing could result in an eviction or loss of a job."[38]

Another problem is that many law enforcement agencies do not report hate crime incidents at all. In many states, it is not considered a hate crime to attack someone because of their sexual orientation or gender identity. According to the Movement Advancement Project, over half of all LGBTQ adults in the US live in these states.

The Red Pill

As people get drawn into the orbit of far-right ideologies, they often refer to having taken the "red pill." The idea of a red pill comes from the science fiction movie *The Matrix*. The hero of the movie, Neo, is presented with a red pill that will free him from society's illusions and allow him to see the world as it truly is. "This is your last chance," the rebel leader tells Neo, holding out a blue pill in one hand and a red pill in the other. "You take the blue pill, the story ends, you wake up in your bed and believe whatever you want to believe. You take the red pill, you stay in Wonderland and I show you how deep the rabbit hole goes."

Initially, the Red Pill was the name of a misogynistic online community hosted on Reddit. By taking the red pill, men would be awakened to the "conspiracies" of feminism. But the red pill metaphor quickly spread throughout the far-right universe. The term was even turned into a verb— to be red-pilled means that one's eyes have been opened to a new way of thinking. "Those who have been red-pilled feel that they have seen the world as it really is and can never go back," posted a member of the alt-right. Ryan Milner, who teaches communications at the College of Charleston, says, "That [red pill] metaphor is so resonant because it has an empowering tenor. You're being awakened, unlocking your power."

Quoted in Emma Grey Ellis, "How Red-Pill Culture Jumped the Fence and Got to Kanye West," *Wired*, April 27, 2018. www.wired.com.

Angela Nagle, "The Lost Boys," *The Atlantic*, December 2017. www.theatlantic.com.

Quoted in Ellis, "How Red-Pill Culture Jumped the Fence and Got to Kanye West."

Economic Uncertainty

The anxiety that some whites feel about losing status and identity to nonwhites, women, and the LGBTQ community has been sharpened by recent changes in the global economy. The term *globalization* refers to the free flow of information, people, and trade across international borders. The effects of globalization have been uneven. While it has made some people rich and has raised about 1 billion people out of poverty in developing countries, the middle and working classes in the developed world have struggled. "Household incomes and wages are stagnant or losing ground for all but the top tier of earners,"[39] according to the Brookings Institution. This has resulted in feelings of hopelessness for many working- and middle-class people, who believe that the current system has lost its legitimacy.

When people lose faith in the system they are living under, they look elsewhere for solutions. Leaders of the alt-right and other extremist movements have used the resentment created by globalization to nurture economic, cultural, and racial nationalism. Nationalism is the opposite of globalization. It means that people should only identify with their own country instead of the world. Nationalism can be a force for good or bad. For example, by uniting people, nationalism helped defeat fascism and communism in the twentieth century. But when nationalism is tied to ethnic claims, it has led to great horrors, such as the Holocaust in Nazi Germany.

Many of today's far-right extremists advocate for a nationalism based on race and ethnicity. They are against multiculturalism and believe that people should only belong to communities that share an ethnic and cultural identity. Meanwhile, they view globalization as a conspiracy of elite, powerful people—usually including Jews—whose goal is to weaken Western heritage while empowering Jews, immigrants, and other minorities. "People are losing their compass," observes Dan Dinar, a Hebrew University historian. "A worldwide stock market, a new form of money, no borders. Concepts like country, nationality, everything is in doubt. They are looking for the ones who are guilty for this new situation and they find the Jews."[40]

However, there is one aspect of globalization that has been embraced by the alt-right and other extremists—its technological benefits. The internet has provided extremists with a powerful tool for propaganda. It also allows them to move money around quickly and anonymously in order to fund people and organizations. It might seem ironic that these nationalists are using the internet—a symbol of globalization, tolerance, and openness—to promote an agenda of hate and extremism. But, as Jamie Bartlett

In 1988 only 11.6 percent of Americans thought that same-sex couples should have the right to marry. Today, that number is 68 percent, and in 2015 the Supreme Court legalized same-sex marriage throughout the United States.

writes in the *Guardian*, "the radical right has frequently been the most avid and enthusiastic adopters of shiny new technology, and have long found the internet a uniquely useful place."[41]

Lack of Faith in Media and Government

Globalization has created great uncertainty for many people. One of the results of this uncertainty is a loss of faith in government, mainstream media, and other institutions. According to the communications marketing firm Edelman, which regularly publishes a so-called Trust Barometer, only one in three Americans in 2018 trusted their government to act appropriately. This was a steep decline from the previous year. Trust in the media also dropped five percentage points, and trust in business dropped ten percentage points.

Never before has Edelman reported such large drops in trust in the United States. Americans are now the least-trusting people of the twenty-eight countries that the firm surveyed. Edelman says the attitude of many respondents was "'I'm not sure about the future of my job because of robots or globalization. I'm not sure about my community anymore because there are a lot of new people coming in. I'm not sure about my economic future; in fact, it looks fairly dim because I'm downwardly mobile."[42]

When people feel uncertain and lose faith in traditional institutions, they sometimes turn to alternative antiestablishment viewpoints. Over the past few years, a large number of young people, most of them white men, have turned to far-right ideologies that rely on alternative theories to "explain" the world. These ideologies appeal to people who are anxiously searching for more certainty and something to believe in. According to writer Angela Nagle, "The far right expertly pinpointed the existential questions, particularly for those who couldn't be permitted a collective identity, namely straight white men: Who are we? What is our story? What is our future?"[43]

CHAPTER THREE

Spreading Hate Through the Internet

On the night of June 17, 2015, a young white man named Dylann Roof walked into an African Methodist Episcopal church in Charleston, South Carolina, during a prayer service. He shot and killed nine people, all of whom were black. According to prosecutors, Roof adopted his white supremacist beliefs from the internet through a "self-learning process" that led him to believe "that violent action is necessary to fight for white people and achieve white supremacy."[44]

Like many others who commit violent hate crimes, Roof engaged with extreme content online. The internet attracts white supremacists like Roof for a few reasons. First, it allows them to operate anonymously. This is important because identifying as an extremist can result in job loss, unpopularity, and even arrest. The internet also allows extremists to reach a broad, worldwide audience, which makes it easier to find like-minded people. And having such a broad audience makes it easier to target and indoctrinate new followers—often using mainstream social media platforms.

Of course, hate and racism existed long before the internet, but today's online platforms allow extremists to promote their propaganda in unprecedented ways. In fact, white supremacists recognized the unique power of the internet a long time ago. "It goes back as far as the '80s," says Daryle Lamont Jenkins, the founder of One People's Project (an organization that monitors far-right groups). "I remember Aryan Nations was some of the first to start using the internet . . . then the general public came on in '95. White supremacists have been using the internet to disseminate their views for that long."[45]

The Dark Side of the Internet

Much of the world is now on social media, with almost a third of the world's population on Facebook alone. In 2019 there were 3.2 billion social media users. That is about 42 percent of the world's population. And that number is only expected to grow.

Social media has changed the way we live, especially the way we get our news and how we communicate with our friends and family. For many, social media is an integral part of their lives. But there is a dark side to this technology. The very features that help people communicate with each other are exploited by far-right groups that seek to spread racial hate, divisive ideas, and mistrust. Even the creators of the internet are aware they may have unleashed a technology that is causing a lot of harm. The inventor of the World Wide Web, Tim Berners-Lee, says, "Humanity connected by technology on the web is functioning in a dystopian way. We have online abuse, prejudice, bias, polarization, fake news, there are lots of ways in which it is broken."[46]

> "Humanity connected by technology on the web is functioning in a dystopian way. We have online abuse, prejudice, bias, polarization, fake news, there are lots of ways in which it is broken."[46]
>
> —Tim Berners-Lee, inventor of the World Wide Web

The internet can make it harder to tell what is and is not true—where the boundaries between fact, opinion, and misinformation lie. One leading think tank has coined the term *truth decay* to describe how social media and political polarization have created

a situation in which many people do not agree on facts anymore, making it difficult for democracies to function properly. "The life-blood of democracy is a common understanding of the facts and information that we can then use as a basis for negotiation and for compromise," says researcher David Bersoff. "When that goes away, the whole foundation of democracy gets shaken."[47]

It was not always this way. The internet was supposed to em-power ordinary citizens and provide a forum for conversation and engagement. But one of the biggest strengths of the internet—its democratic nature—has also turned out to be a weakness. A *New York Times* book reviewer provides an example of this in her piece about Andrew Marantz's book *Antisocial*. One of the people described by Marantz, the reviewer writes, is a "60-year-old 'surly racist' with 25,000 subscribers on YouTube who, in another era, might have been relegated to muttering on his front porch."[48]

Most internet users are dismayed and upset by this growing wave of toxic rage. In 2018 the Anti-Defamation League (ADL) conducted a survey and found that 37 percent of Americans have experienced severe online harassment. This includes sex-ual harassment, physical threats, stalking, and other forms of

The Dark Web

There is a part of the internet that most people do not know about. It is not even visible to search engines. It is called the dark web. True to its name, the dark web is a pretty shady place. It is a marketplace for all kinds of illegal things: drugs, guns, counterfeit money, hacking software, stolen credit card numbers, and child pornography.

Buyers pay for things on the dark web with cryptocurrencies like bitcoin, which allow people to make financial transactions anonymously. But this does not mean that it is safe to do business here. Many dark websites are set up by scammers and thieves. Many buyers have also been arrested or jailed for attempted purchases of illegal products and materials.

Not surprisingly, the dark web is a refuge for many white supremacists who have had their websites banned by mainstream service providers. On the dark web they can post extreme material anonymously and without fear of reprisal. One popular message board that gets half a million visits a month features discussion threads such as "What do you want done with the Jews?"

Not all the dark web is bad. In fact, it serves a valuable service by helping thousands of people communicate anonymously online in places where free speech is restricted. "A lot of people use it in countries where there's eavesdropping or where internet access is criminalized," says security expert Patrick Tiquet.

Quoted in Darren Guccione, "What Is the Dark Web? How to Access It and What You'll Find," CSO, July 4, 2019. www.csoonline.com.

harassment. This figure is substantially higher than the 18 percent reported in 2017 by the Pew Research Center. This sharp increase startled Adam Neufeld, the ADL's vice president of innovation and strategy. "This was significantly worse than we expected,"[49] he says.

How Hate Spreads Online

The internet is highly effective at spreading information, but problems can arise when that information is false or misleading. In late 2016 some people used social media sites like Reddit to spread a rumor that Democrats, including Hillary Clinton, were running a child sex operation out of a pizzeria in Washington, DC. This conspiracy theory became known as Pizzagate. As the story spread, the owner of the pizzeria received death threats, and a man with an assault rifle fired a shot inside the restaurant. No one was hurt.

The quick spread of the Pizzagate conspiracy theory around the internet is an example of something going viral. This is when thousands and even millions of people share a piece of news, an image, or a video. Studies have shown that people tend to share more when they feel angry. "Anger is a high-arousal emotion, which drives people to take action," says Jonah Berger, a professor at the University of Pennsylvania's Wharton School. Anger "makes you feel fired up, which makes you more likely to pass things on."[50]

It is not just people that share and spread hateful messages—it is computer algorithms. Algorithms are a way of sorting information to predict what a user might be interested in, but they can also inadvertently promote extreme content. One example is YouTube's autoplay function. With autoplay, another video automatically starts playing after the first one finishes. Many have criticized the YouTube algorithm for recommending a succession of videos that can quickly take users to dark corners of the internet. "For a 14-year-old who may stumble on some sort of a propaganda video, they'll be fed more of those videos," says Christian Picciolini, the founder of Life After Hate. "And essentially, the internet and the algorithms are working to radicalize us if we land in the wrong place."[51]

One solution to this problem is for social media platforms to crack down on objectionable material. For example, Reddit banned the so-called Pizzagate thread from its site. But social media sites risk losing customers and revenue if they ban speech too broadly. In 2019 a Bloomberg investigation found that YouTube executives were unwilling to take down many extreme and misleading videos because they were too focused on achieving their business goal—increasing viewing time and user engagement.

Normalizing Hate

Thanks to the internet, hateful ideologies can now spread faster and further than ever before, creating an impression that these ideas are more mainstream and commonplace than they really are. The more people are exposed to irrational ideas, the more acceptable these ideas can become. "A lot of our behavior is driven by what we think other people do and what other people find acceptable,"[52] says Nour Kteily, an associate professor at Northwestern University's Kellogg School of Management. For example, a 2015 study showed that the more people were exposed to homophobic slurs, the more they tended to rate gay people as less human.

"A lot of our behavior is driven by what we think other people do and what other people find acceptable."[52]

—Nour Kteily, associate professor of management and organizations at Northwestern University's Kellogg School of Management

Portraying people as less than human is called dehumanization. This is a common tactic among far-right hate groups because dehumanizing people makes it easier to commit violence against them. For this reason, social media sites try to eliminate dehumanizing speech. "Language that makes someone less than human can have repercussions off the service, including normalizing serious violence,"[53] Twitter employees wrote in a 2018 post announcing a proposed policy change.

Researchers are still trying to understand the different ways that social media can normalize hate and violence. One study reported that antirefugee attacks in Germany were more likely to occur in towns with more usage of Facebook—a platform that often features antirefugee sentiment. One of the authors of the study, Carlo Schwarz from the University of Warwick, says that there are some people "who seem to be pushed toward violent acts by the exposure to online hate speech." When people are

YouTube's autoplay automatically starts playing another video after one video finishes. Many have criticized this algorithm for recommending a succession of videos that can quickly take users to dark corners of the internet.

repeatedly exposed to the same hateful ideas, he says, it may change their perception about "how acceptable it is to commit acts of violence against minority groups."[54]

Reinforcing Hate

Not only can the internet make hateful ideas seem more normal and acceptable, it can also strengthen belief in those ideas. Researchers have found that spending long amounts of time with people who agree with you reinforces belief in the most extreme opinions. "If you want to make people more extreme, you don't

Manifestos

Many far-right extremists who commit mass murder leave behind manifestos. A manifesto is a published declaration of the writer's intentions, motives, or views. Because of recent attacks, many people associate manifestos with extreme and violent ideologies, but manifestos can present a wide variety of ideas. The Declaration of Independence, for example, is a manifesto.

The manifestos left behind by the shooters in El Paso, Christchurch, and Pittsburgh all provide an ideological rationale for mass murder. Each of these shootings was designed to go viral. The shooter's horrific actions would catch everyone's attention, then the shooter's manifesto would deliver a hate-filled payload. By leaving these manifestos behind, the shooters were adding to a long and growing library of terror. "They're also trying to inspire others about the urgency of the moment. . . . You see these ideas building on each other," says Heidi Beirich, director of the SPLC's Intelligence Project. "There's no question these people are feeding off each other because they're referencing prior manifestos."

Unfortunately, when the news media reports about mass shootings, the hateful ideas contained in the manifestos are sometimes amplified. That is one of the reasons manifestos have become a valuable tool for extremists hoping to inspire more attacks. According to Clint Watts of the Foreign Policy Research Institute, when potential shooters hear about an attack and read the manifesto, "they mobilize because they want to get into the media storm. They want to be part of that phenomenon. It becomes a contagion."

Quoted in Kelly Weill, "From El Paso to Christchurch, a Racist Lie Is Fueling Terrorist Attacks," Daily Beast, August 4, 2019. www.thedailybeast.com.

have to threaten them or brainwash them. Just plop them in a like-minded group, and human nature will do the rest,"[55] writes Derek Thompson, a journalist who covers technology and the media for the *Atlantic*.

A famous experiment measuring the power of groups was conducted in the 1970s. Hundreds of college undergraduates were divided into two groups according to how liberal or conservative they were. The students in each group were then left alone to talk for a while. Afterward, researchers were able to determine that after spending time with people who shared their views, the conservative students had become much more conservative, while the liberal students had become considerably more liberal.

> "If you want to make people more extreme, you don't have to threaten them or brainwash them. Just plop them in a like-minded group, and human nature will do the rest."[55]
>
> —Derek Thompson, a journalist who covers technology and the media

In some ways, social media platforms are re-creating this experiment on a vastly larger scale. The internet allows people to find other people who are just like them while excluding people who are different. This tends to inhibit learning and tolerance for cultural diversity. Professor Jason Chan from the University of Minnesota has studied how the online world reinforces hate in the real world. He explains, "The likely reason behind this is the Internet facilitates this specialization of interest. That is to say, users will search out content online that is congruent to their beliefs or preferences and are not as likely to look up content that is counter to what they believe in."[56]

Publicizing Hate

On March 15, 2019, a shooter entered two separate mosques in Christchurch, New Zealand, and killed fifty-one worshippers who had gathered to pray. In addition to semiautomatic rifles and shotguns, the shooter also used the tools of the internet as weapons in his deadly attack. Before entering the first mosque, the shooter had posted a seventy-four-page manifesto online. He then strapped a camera to his forehead and streamed a live video of the attack on Facebook for seventeen minutes.

The shooter's video was widely available on sites like Facebook, Twitter, and YouTube until the postings were taken down. In the first twenty-four hours after the attack, Facebook alone removed 1.5 million postings of the video. Sociologist Joan Donovan of the Harvard University Kennedy School of Government writes, "The extra

Syrian refugees walk in a train station after arriving in Germany in 2015. Studies have shown that antirefugee attacks were more likely to occur in towns with more usage of Facebook—a platform that often features antirefugee sentiment.

attention that these ideas gain in the aftermath of a violent attack isn't just an unfortunate side effect of news coverage. It's the sound system by which extremist movements transmit their ideas to a broader public, and they are using it with more and more skill."[57]

Research has shown that most shooters are in fact inspired by other shooters. Mass killings are socially contagious and tend to come in clusters. The shooting in El Paso, Texas, for example, happened in the same week as two other mass shootings—one in Dayton, Ohio, and the other in Gilroy, California. For the Christchurch shooter, the internet was by far the most effective way to document and publicize his actions in the hope of inspiring others to carry out similar attacks. "There is no doubt in my mind that this guy was very aware of how his video and his manifesto would filter through the internet and get refracted and picked up and analyzed," says Kevin Roose of the *New York Times*. "This was, in a way, engineered for internet virality."[58]

Targeting Teens

According to Common Sense Media, teenagers today spend an average of nine hours a day online. This allows them plenty of opportunity to interact with undesirable material—sometimes in unexpected ways. In March 2019 an eighteen-year-old high school senior in Washington State was on the popular gaming chat platform Discord, which white supremacists have sometimes used to promote their ideas. Suddenly, news broke about someone shooting people in mosques in New Zealand. The student was quickly able to find the shooter's Instagram account and jokingly wrote a message in the style of white supremacists: "War is on the horizon we shall not lose we shall survive!" Much to his dismay, an answer came back: "This is my final message, this is my farewell." Then the account shut down. "I did make a stupid decision," the student said later. At the time, he thought, "Oh, God, I just messaged the shooter!"[59]

Discord, which has 250 million users, is just one example of how easy it is for adolescents to access and become involved with extremist material on the internet. This kind of material can appeal to young people who often feel out of place, misunderstood, and uncertain of who they are. "We are talking about young people who don't yet have full-formed opinions and worldviews," says Lindsay Schubiner, program director at Western States Center. "It is for that very reason that extremists often try to target them."[60]

Today 89 percent of teens own smartphones, compared to only 41 percent in 2012. Nearly two-thirds report coming across hate speech or other content on social media. But gaming platforms like Discord offer white supremacists a particularly effective way to recruit teenagers—especially white male teenagers.

"Recruiters go to where targets are, staging seemingly casual conversations about issues of race and identity in spaces where lots of disaffected, vulnerable adolescent white males tend to hang out,"[61] says Megan Condisa, assistant professor of game studies at Texas Tech University.

Some people believe that online gamers who fall prey to white supremacist ideology do not pose a physical threat. They argue that people like neo-Nazis or skinheads are much more capable of violence. But others disagree. One former white supremacist says, "It's a really big error to discount those people. They turn into the school shooters, the bombers. . . . Look at Dylann Roof. He went seamlessly from the internet to murder."[62]

The senior from Washington State who messaged the New Zealand shooter did not get into any serious trouble for his actions. But the FBI did show up. "They asked me if I had any idea why they were there and I said that I had a pretty good idea," says the senior, who called the whole incident a life lesson. He said he realizes now how vulnerable teenagers are to those trying to exploit them. "People our age are susceptible to a lot of things,"[63] he says.

CHAPTER FOUR

Leaving Hate and Extremism Behind

Shane Johnson was born into a KKK family in Indiana. From a very early age, he was taught to hate. "They believe that everybody else is subhuman—that they don't have a soul, and only white people do,"[64] he says. In seventh grade Johnson dropped out of school to dedicate himself to the KKK, eventually rising in the ranks to become one of the organization's leaders.

After brutally attacking an interracial couple enjoying an outdoor concert, Johnson woke up the next day in jail. His fists were cut up and bruised, and his neck and back ached from being kneed, punched, and Tasered by the police. Johnson began to wonder what he was doing with his life and decided to leave the KKK. But how? He had a lengthy criminal record; no skills, job, or money; and white supremacist tattoos covering his entire body. "I just decided, I got to figure out—Who am I?" says Johnson, "What is going on with me?"[65]

Trying to Escape Hate

Johnson is not alone. As the number of hate groups have surged, so have the number of people trying to leave them. But there are few places they can turn to for help. In order to fill this need, a group of former white supremacists founded Life After Hate in 2011. According to the group's mission statement, "Life After Hate is committed to helping people leave the violent far-right to connect with humanity and lead compassionate lives. . . . We do this through education, interventions, academic research, and outreach."[66]

Arno Michaels is one of the cofounders of Life After Hate. Growing up in a comfortable Milwaukee suburb, Michaels discovered he had a taste for violence. By age sixteen he was a racist skinhead filled with hate for anybody who was not white or heterosexual. For seven years Michaels enjoyed the drunken, brawling skinhead lifestyle. But when his daughter was born, he began to dream of a different kind of life for her. "The only people I could interact with were other racist white people," he recalls. He also started getting involved in the rave scene, and found himself dancing with people of different races. "It was getting more and more difficult to deny the humanity of the people I was supposed to hate."[67] Today the memories of the savage beatings he gave innocent people haunt him like a ghost, he says.

> "It was getting more and more difficult to deny the humanity of the people I was supposed to hate."[67]
>
> —Arno Michaels, cofounder of Life After Hate

Angela King is another cofounder of Life After Hate. Raised in a strictly conservative, religious family in southern Florida, King had a secret she did not dare share with anyone. "From very early on I felt I was abnormal because I was attracted to people of the same sex,"[68] King says. This secret left her confused, angry, and resentful. She was getting into fights at school and soon realized that violence gave her a sense of control she had not experienced before. After her parents divorced, King joined a group of teenagers who were starting to become involved with neo-Nazism. "I joined them because they accepted my violence and anger without question."[69]

Soon after, the group robbed a video store, and King was arrested and sent to prison for her involvement. While in prison, she

Raising Money to Fight Hate

Just before leaving office, former president Barack Obama awarded a $400,000 grant to Life After Hate. But soon after taking office, incoming president Donald Trump revoked the grant. "We never got an explanation for why our grant was rescinded," said Christian Picciolini, one of the cofounders of the organization. One government official said the grant may have been revoked because Picciolini had criticized Trump on Twitter.

The organizations that did receive grants to fight extremism from the Trump administration were ones that focused exclusively on Islamist extremists. Government officials downplayed the danger posed by far-right extremists, despite research showing that white supremacist groups have been responsible for most domestic terrorist attacks recently. On a radio show, presidential adviser Sebastian Gorka said, "It's this constant, 'Oh, it's the white man. It's the white supremacists. That's the problem.' No, it isn't."

Life After Hate was not the only group that lost its funding. A University of North Carolina program dedicated to fighting against white supremacist recruiting and Islamist extremism lost a nearly $900,000 grant. "There is a very clear signal that the only threat this administration is interested in regarding violent extremism is the radical Islamic threat," says John D. Cohen, a former US Department of Homeland Security adviser. Despite losing the grant, Life After Hate was able to raise over $400,000 after the 2017 Unite the Right rally in Charlottesville, Virginia, including a $50,000 donation by football quarterback and civil rights activist Colin Kaepernick.

Quoted in Ron Nixon and Eileen Sullivan, "Revocation of Grants to Help Fight Hate Under New Scrutiny After Charlottesville," *New York Times*, August 15, 2017. www.nytimes.com.

met people from different cultures and backgrounds for the first time. Much to her surprise, King eventually fell in love with a Jamaican woman. Upon her release, King was determined to change her life. She attended a community college and studied sociology and psychology.

In 2011 she went to an international conference, where she met Michaels and other former extremists. The group decided to found Life After Hate, which has grown to include thousands of people across the globe. "I was excited to meet other people who had got involved in violent extremism and then got out. I wasn't alone,"[70] King says.

The Path to Extremism

In order to help people leave extremist hate groups, it is important to understand their motivations for joining in the first place. To do this, Norwegian sociologist Tore Bjørgo interviewed white supremacists as they tried to leave neo-Nazi groups. His findings were unexpected. Most of the people he interviewed became hard-core racists only *after* they had joined an extremist group. Instead of racism, it was a mixture of experiences such as childhood abuse, depression, anxiety, and isolation that led them to join. Research backs this up: a 2016 study from the University of Maryland showed that the most common factor among those who join violent extremist groups is emotional trauma. Life After Hate cofounder Tony McAleer calls it "toxic shame. We pick up the belief that we aren't lovable enough, smart enough, that we're powerless and weak" and extremist groups can offer "a sense of belonging, a sense of camaraderie, meaning, and significance."[71]

The University of Maryland study pinpointed three factors that lead to radicalization: they are called the three Ns—need, narrative, and network. Hate groups satisfy the powerful need to belong to a greater cause, the racist ideology provides the narrative, and fellow extremists are the network.

What these findings show is that the process of deradicalizing extremists is mostly about helping them find a new, constructive set of the three Ns. For Michaels, the path to deradicalization began with the birth of his daughter. For King, it was meeting a group of Jamaican women in prison and falling in love with one of them. Johnson was finally able to leave the KKK by focusing on a new cause—the fight against hate and extremism. "I'm blessed with the opportunity to get the message out there," he says, "and all I can do is humble myself and tell the . . . truth. I believe the truth can keep people from joining."[72]

Engaging with Hate

People who successfully leave hate groups are known as formers, short for "former violent extremists." Because of their own experiences, formers are particularly effective at knowing how to help someone exit from a hate group. Formers say that trying to show extremists how wrong they are is one of the least effective ways to reach them. "Rather than shaming them as living dark, hate-filled lives," says Johnson, "you need to challenge them to engage."[73]

For many extremists who try to leave hate groups, the process begins when someone sees them for who they are, not for the terrible things they did. Life After Hate cofounder Christian Picciolini says that deradicalization is not about debating

Former right-wing extremist Christian Picciolini speaks to an audience at Temple Israel in Minneapolis in 2017. Picciolini is a cofounder of Life After Hate, an organization committed to helping people leave the violent far-right to live more compassionate lives.

or confronting people about their ideology—it is more about creating a rapport. Picciolini explains:

It's a whole lot of listening. I listen for what I call potholes: things that happen to us in our journey of life that detour us, things like trauma, abuse, mental illness, poverty, joblessness. . . . Nobody's born racist; we all found it. . . . People hate other people because they hate something very specifically about themselves, or are very angry about a situation within their own environment, and that is then projected onto other people. So I'm really trying to build resilience with people.[74]

Another important experience for people trying to leave hate groups is meeting and socially interacting with someone they are supposed to hate. For people who might already be questioning their worldview, these encounters can be a revelation as their crude stereotypes dissolve. Sociologist Michael Kimmel reports that many former white supremacists report meeting "a member of the despised group, one singular individual whose very existence eroded all their categorical group stereotypes, [and] they began to unlearn the dehumanization the movement had taught them."[75] Life After Hate tries to create and encourage these types of encounters by bringing white supremacists to mosques and events like break dancing competitions. Some people have criticized this technique because it can imply that victimized groups are somehow responsible for helping "save" their oppressors, but it remains an effective tool.

> "People hate other people because they hate something very specifically about themselves, or are very angry about a situation within their own environment, and that is then projected onto other people."[74]
>
> —Christian Picciolini, cofounder of Life After Hate

Some formers admit it can be exhausting playing therapist for white supremacists. Continually responding to hate and violence

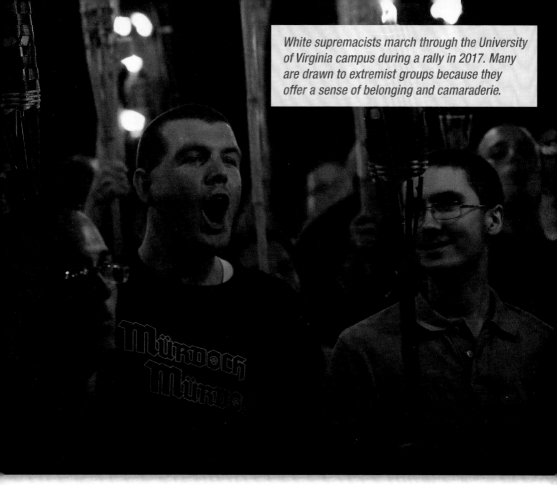

White supremacists march through the University of Virginia campus during a rally in 2017. Many are drawn to extremist groups because they offer a sense of belonging and camaraderie.

with love and compassion is a challenge, but they say the results are worth it. The key to success, according to Pardeep Singh Kaleka, cofounder of Serve 2 Unite (a program that promotes unity among young people), is that "we have to make it clear we cannot vilify racists, but we can vilify racism."[76]

Addicted to Hate

Leaving a life of hate and extremism behind can be a very long and difficult process. People cannot just turn off the hate so easily. In fact, some experts now believe that the process of deradicalization can be likened to a struggle against addiction. A recent study found that violence can trigger a brain response like the one triggered by drug use. This response wears

> "We have to make it clear we cannot vilify racists, but we can vilify racism."[76]
>
> —Pardeep Singh Kaleka, cofounder of Serve 2 Unite

Erasing the Hate

One thing that may stand in the way of individuals trying to change their lives after leaving a hate group is the racist tattoos that cover their bodies. Former violent extremists are often desperate to remove these reminders of their former selves, but covering up a tattoo is more complicated than getting the original. It takes time, it is painful, and it is expensive.

Most people cannot afford the costs, so some tattoo artists have started doing cover-ups for free. Dave Cutlip, who runs a tattoo parlor in Maryland, started doing free cover-ups after a man came in hoping to get a racist tattoo removed from his face. "I could see the hurt in his eyes," Cutlip said. Most of the tattoos people want covered up are swastikas, pictures of Hitler, and words such as *Aryan or skinhead*. In order to make tattoo cover-ups more accessible to people, Cutlip and his wife started a crowdfunding effort for the Random Acts of Tattoo Project. The money raised goes to tattoo artists who cannot afford to work for free, including those with training in laser tattoo removal.

Many tattoo artists are willing to donate their time because they believe they are making a positive difference. "You rarely get that opportunity to change someone's life," says tattoo artist Drew Darby. "That's why I do stuff like this as a tattoo artist. Because when the opportunity occasionally presents itself, you have to take it."

Quoted in Justin Wm. Moyer, "'Sometimes People Change': Maryland Shop Covers Up People's Racist Tattoos for Free," *Washington Post*, February 22, 2017. www.washingtonpost.com.

Quoted in Deborah Bloom, "Erasing the Hate: The Tattoo Shop Offering Former White Supremacists a Fresh Start," *The Guardian* (Manchester), February 5, 2019. www.theguardian.com.

off quickly, so if you are addicted to hate, you must constantly experience hateful thoughts, actions, and words in order to "get a hit." Extremists may engage in violence or listen to hate music not only to reinforce their beliefs but to get a high out of the experience. "I can listen to white-power music and within a week be back in that mindset," a former neo-Nazi says. "I guarantee you it's an addiction."[77]

After Johnson left the KKK and embraced a totally new life, he sometimes wondered whether he had really changed at all. He still could not read the Bible without seeing evidence that nonwhites did not have souls and that God demanded their enslavement. Sometimes when he saw a mixed-race couple, the words *race traitor* popped into his mind. "It's kind of like a drug addiction," he says. "You have to admit you have a problem to fix the problem."[78] One study showed that dozens of formers reported having unwanted racist thoughts. Sometimes they even acted on them, seemingly against their will. One woman said she flew into a rage in a restaurant, called a Hispanic a racial slur, and then gave the Nazi salute—all before she even realized what she was doing.

If research continues to reveal a connection between extremism and addiction, the deradicalization process might become more like a twelve-step program, similar to Alcoholics Anonymous. Just as Alcoholics Anonymous members must manage their desire to drink, former extremists would need to man-

> "It took me less than two years to learn to hate, and it took me nine years to unlearn it."[79]
>
> —A former member of a paramilitary group

age their violent, racist urges. Regardless, breaking away from hate and extremism can be an arduous journey. "It took me less than two years to learn to hate," a former member of a paramilitary group says, "and it took me nine years to unlearn it."[79]

The Difficulties of Leaving Extremism

Another reason people find it difficult to leave hate groups is because the lifestyle is so all-consuming. An extremist is an extremist each and every day. Hate infuses every aspect of the person's life. "People in extremist groups wrap their entire identities around it," says King. When they decide to leave, "everything in their life has to be changed, from the way they think, to the people they associate with, to dealing with permanent tattoos."[80]

Many formers report feeling a tremendous void in their lives after leaving a hate group. Even becoming a former who counsels others does not necessarily fill that void. Life After Hate cofounder Frank Meeink says it was terrible to feel so alone and powerless after years of living in a hate-filled fantasy surrounded by fellow extremists. Even after becoming an acclaimed public speaker, he started doing heroin, and his life fell apart. "I couldn't stand to be me, unfiltered, unprotected. . . . I never had the guts to take a searching and fearless moral inventory of myself."[81]

To make matters worse, people are often violently punished for leaving a hate group. One former member of the Aryan Brotherhood was shot in the face and lost his right eye and most of the sight in his left. When Johnson decided to leave the KKK, he knew he was antagonizing his family by switching sides. One day a group of men attacked Johnson in a parking lot. They smashed both eye sockets, cracked his jaw, and knocked out several teeth. They also broke his leg, an ankle, both wrists, most of his fingers, his nose, and all his ribs. His right eardrum was ruptured, and he will never hear on that side again. Leaving a hate group is "not something where you can just say: 'I've changed my mind,'" says King. "There are serious and oftentimes violent repercussions for trying to walk away from something like that."[82]

Change Is Possible

Despite the difficulties people face when trying to leave a hate group, change is possible. Many former extremists have changed their lives in substantial and sometimes surprising ways. One former extremist says, "When people who know me today find out I used to be a neo-Nazi, they can't believe it; and when people I used to be associated with as a neo-Nazi find out who I am today, they can't believe it either."[83]

Many formers report that one of the difficult hurdles to overcome when trying to change is forgiving themselves for the harm they have done to others. King says the process of forgiving herself is slow and painful. But it is necessary work, especially if she hopes to help others change their lives. "I have a lot of healthy guilt about who I was and the things I did to hurt others and myself. But I know I would not have been able to do this work had I not had those experiences,"[84] she says.

The deradicalization process can be a difficult adjustment. Seeing a mixed-race couple can easily trigger ingrained emotional reactions for those trying to leave the extremist life.

Michaels often tells his story to students and young people all over the country, hoping to promote the notion of basic human goodness. He tells them how difficult it is for him to think about the terrible things he did when he was younger. But he was able to change, and now he is a different man, a tolerant person who respects diversity. "I attacked a gay man because I was drunk," he tells students. "I broke his face. And I laughed about it. That was almost 20 years ago. I'll never forget that night. But I have the power to transform that act of stupidity into something positive, and I can share that with you guys, to hope that you can learn from my mistakes."[85]

Michaels's message of tolerance and hope resonates with young people who are struggling to find camaraderie, meaning, and significance in their lives. There is nothing noble or challenging about choosing to hate, Michaels tells them. The real challenge is learning how to respond to aggression with compassion. Students are listening to his message. After hearing Michaels speak, one student wrote, "I've been asked to and have done things I'm not proud of. Before you came, I was thinking about going back to my old ways. But you . . . showed me I can accomplish great things. Thank you for planting this positive seed."[86]

CHAPTER FIVE

Responding to Hate and Extremism

On August 5, 2012, a man named Wade Page walked into a Sikh temple in Oak Creek, Wisconsin, and opened fire, killing six people. Later, sociologist Pete Simi was about to appear on a major cable news show to talk about the shooting. Before the show, a producer asked him why Page had not been arrested earlier, since it was known that he played in a neo-Nazi band. Simi was taken aback by the question. "Of course, I explained that being in a neo-Nazi music band wasn't against the law, nor were the neo-Nazi tattoos Page had inscribed on his body, nor were his neo-Nazi beliefs,"[87] says Simi.

Hate speech generally is protected by law under the First Amendment of the US Constitution. But not all hate speech is protected. For example, speech that incites a crowd to violence is illegal. Symbols of hate, such as swastikas and burning crosses, are also protected under the First Amendment. But, again, not all the time. They are not protected if they directly threaten someone or if they desecrate private property. Plus, it is important to remember that the First Amendment only protects speech from government censorship. Businesses, schools, and other private entities are not constrained by constitutional free speech laws.

Today, as society struggles to find effective ways to combat the spread of hate and extremism, the fact that hateful speech and symbols are often legally protected angers and frustrates many people. But, as Simi says, it is important to be aware of how the law operates. "I think it's critical we keep the Constitution at the forefront of our discussions when we focus on how to respond to this type of violence."[88]

> "I think it's critical we keep the Constitution at the forefront of our discussions when we focus on how to respond to [hate-based] violence."[88]
>
> —Pete Simi, associate professor in the Department of Sociology at Chapman University

Organizing Against Hate and Extremism

Organizations like Life After Hate, the SPLC, and the ADL play important roles in fighting the spread of hate and extremism. They can educate and raise awareness, monitor and expose hate, seek justice, teach tolerance, and intervene and rehabilitate. Organizations can also offer their members support, advice, and encouragement.

As the number of extremist groups and hate incidents continues to rise, so does the number of organizations dedicated to fighting violence and intolerance. In 2017 Communities Against

Not all hate speech is protected by the Constitution. Symbols of hate such as swastikas (pictured) are not protected if they directly threaten someone or if they desecrate private property.

Hate was launched. This historic coalition of eleven prominent national organizations and neighborhood groups works to address the disturbing rise in hate and extremism across the United States. According to its website, Communities Against Hate allows people "to share stories of hate incidents through our online database and telephone hotline. . . . We connect survivors and witnesses to legal resources and social services. And we come together to advocate for a better America."[89]

That same year, NBCUniversal announced that the company's Emmy-winning Erase the Hate campaign, originally founded in 1994 to combat hate and discrimination in America, would be relaunched. The relaunch was accompanied by a music video starring rapper Princess Nokia and hip-hop artist Timbaland. The campaign also provides grants, coaching, and mentorship to people and organizations acting against hate. "Silence equals complicity," says NBCUniversal chair Bonnie Hammer. "Hate and bias must be called out wherever and whenever we see it. We all have a part to play."[90]

Leading the Fight Against Hate

Perhaps no other individuals have as much power to prevent the spread of hate and violence as the elected leaders of the United States. Immediately following the September 11, 2001, terrorist attacks, there was a wave of anti-Muslim hate crimes. Then, on September 17, President George W. Bush visited an American mosque and made the following remarks: "The face of terrorism is not the true faith of Islam. That's not what Islam is all about. Islam is peace. These terrorists don't represent peace, they represent evil and war. . . . When we think of Islam, we think of a faith that brings comfort to a billion people around the world . . . and that's made brothers and sisters out of every race."[91] Following the presi-

> "The face of terrorism is not the true faith of Islam. That's not what Islam is all about. Islam is peace. These terrorists don't represent peace, they represent evil and war."[91]
>
> —George W. Bush, president of the United States

dent's remarks, anti-Muslim hate crimes dropped dramatically across the country.

In contrast, shortly after a terrorist attack in San Bernardino, California, in 2015, then-candidate Donald Trump called for a ban on Muslims entering the United States. After Trump's remarks, anti-Muslim hate crime rose 87.5 percent. "There's very compelling evidence that political rhetoric may well play a role in directing behavior in the aftermath of a terrorist attack," says Brian Levin, director of the Center for the Study of Hate and Extremism at California State University, San Bernardino. Such "rhetoric is one of the significant variables that can contribute to hate crimes."[92]

> "There's very compelling evidence that political rhetoric may well play a role in directing behavior in the aftermath of a terrorist attack."[92]
>
> —Brian Levin, director of the Center for the Study of Hate and Extremism at California State University, San Bernardino

After a terrorist attack in San Bernardino, California, in 2015, then-candidate Donald Trump (pictured) called for a ban on Muslims entering the United States. After Trump's remarks, anti-Muslim hate crime rose by 87.5 percent.

Policing Hate

If you were to ask police chiefs how many hate crimes have taken place in their communities over the past year, most would probably say very few, if any. But they would most likely be wrong. Officially, a hate crime is reported almost every hour, but almost twenty-five times that number is estimated to occur, according to the Leadership Conference on Civil and Human Rights. "A lot of these law enforcement agencies don't believe that they have a problem with hate crimes," says Roy Austin, a former deputy assistant attorney general of the US Department of Justice. "If they don't think they have a problem, they won't deal with it well."[93]

People do not report hate crimes for a variety of reasons. According to a national survey, most people who believe they were victims of hate were unable to provide evidence that police could use to prove bias. For example, Brandon Ballone, a drag performer, was attacked by a group of men in New York in 2016. They beat him with a bottle, damaging his jaw and severed a tendon in his hand. Ballone said he did not remember whether his attackers called him homophobic names. As a result, police did not consider the attack a hate crime. Many Latinos do not report hate crimes to the police because they are afraid of being deported. "Even if you get robbed or exploited or you're in danger, you just don't want that unnecessary attention,"[94] says Pricila Garcia, the daughter of Mexican immigrants. To confuse matters even more, hate crime laws are widely inconsistent across the United States. Currently, four states—Arkansas, Georgia, South Carolina, and Wyoming—do not have any kind of hate crime law at all.

Because hate crimes appear to be so few in number, law enforcement officers often do not receive the proper training to deal with the problem. To remedy this situation, two advocacy groups have organized a traveling workshop that visits police forces across the country. During the workshop, police officers learn about state and federal laws pertaining to hate crimes, listen to victims of hate incidents, and are asked to debate whether certain scenarios fulfill the legal requirements of a hate crime. Many police officers wel-

Parents for Peace

After growing up in a black, churchgoing family in Memphis, Tennessee, Carlos Bledsoe converted to Islam in college. He changed his name and slowly began drifting toward the extremist fringes of Islam. On June 1, 2009, he shot and killed a US soldier in Arkansas. Today he is serving a life sentence in prison.

His father, Melvin, was totally blindsided by Carlos's transformation. Melvin did not want anyone else to experience the pain of losing a child to violent extremism, so in 2015 he and his daughter Monica Holley founded Parents for Peace. The purpose of the organization is to provide support for families going through the same thing they had gone through. "This is a no-judgment zone," Holley says. "And I think that's the most comforting thing, to know that you can talk to someone and not be judged by what your loved one did."

Parents for Peace began mainly as a support group but started shifting to policy and prevention work in response to the resurgence of hate and extremism. Today the organization is dedicated to reframing extremism as a public health crisis that can affect anyone, regardless of race, religion, or environment. "I'm on a mission," Melvin says. "I want to help others. No one should have to go through the pain. No one."

Quoted in Hannah Allam, "'We Were Blindsided': Families of Extremists Form Group to Fight Hate," NPR, December 12, 2019. www.npr.org.

come the training. "If we don't train, if we don't stay on top of the current changes and laws and the attitudes and the climate, then we're going to pay a big price for that," one veteran officer says. "We'll lose the trust of the community, and we can't do that."[95]

Teaching Tolerance

Reaching young, impressionable people before they choose hate is one of the most important strategies for combating extremism. But many teachers and school administrators do not feel qualified to identify students who might be engaging with extremist material. In response, several organizations are providing tools and guidance to help teachers recognize white supremacist ideology and at-risk students.

The Stress of Human Moderators

Artificial intelligence and algorithms can help tech companies detect and remove hateful content, but these tools are limited in what they can do. For this reason, tens of thousands of people all over the world have been hired to review and delete violent and extremist content. All day long these people are exposed "to people getting hurt, to animals getting hurt, and all sorts of hurtful violent imagery," says Sylvia Estrada-Claudio, who counsels workers in the industry. "For people with underlying issues, it can set off a psychological crisis."

After spending a year moderating terrorism and child abuse material, one woman experienced frequent panic attacks and had difficulty interacting with children without crying. After seeing a psychiatrist, she was diagnosed with post-traumatic stress disorder. Another moderator says, "Every day you watch someone beheading someone, or someone shooting his girlfriend. After that, you feel like wow, this world is really crazy. . . . Why are we doing this to each other?"

Tech company officials say that they had to create these new jobs in a hurry and are still struggling to satisfy society's increasing demands to remove undesirable content while offering appropriate psychological care for their employees. Google's own researchers admit that "there is . . . an increasing awareness and recognition that beyond mere unpleasantness, long-term or extensive viewing of such disturbing content can incur significant health consequences for those engaged in such tasks."

Quoted in Elizabeth Dwoskin et al., "Content Moderators at YouTube, Facebook and Twitter See the Worst of the Web—and Suffer Silently," *Washington Post*, July 25, 2019. www.washingtonpost.com.

Quoted in Casey Newton, "The Terror Queue," The Verge, December 16, 2019. www.theverge.com.

Quoted in Newton, "The Terror Queue."

Teaching Tolerance was founded by the SPLC to prevent the growth of hate in schools. It provides free resources, including films and a magazine, to educators who work with children and high school students. Today its community includes more than five hundred thousand educators. The materials produced by Teaching Tolerance have won two Oscars, an Emmy, and many other honors.

Another organization for educators is Western States Center, based in Portland, Oregon. It has published a forty-seven-page manual to help teachers confront extremism. "What we heard from teachers, administrators and educators is that they were just not quite sure what to do,"[96] says Eric Ward, executive director of Western States Center. The manual trains teachers about a variety of situations, like what to do if a teacher finds a swastika carved into a desk or if a student makes a white power gesture. It also features a list of common racist symbols.

But the question of how effective these school programs are is debated. Former FBI agent Michael German says that he is all for teaching tolerance but says there is not much evidence that these programs work. "The idea of these programs was that if they could suppress the bad ideas there would be less violence, but there's no evidence that this is true,"[97] he says.

Removing Hate from the Internet

Nowhere has hate and extremism spread more effectively and rapidly than on the internet. In response, technology companies like YouTube, Facebook, and Twitter have been under intense pressure to remove hateful content and disinformation from their platforms. From April through June 2019, YouTube says it removed over 100,000 videos, 17,000 channels, and 500 million comments for violating its terms on hate speech. This was five times more content than it had removed in the previous three months. At the same time, Facebook closed down a number of accounts belonging to extremist figures. "It's been a very long few years of getting platform companies to understand the role that digital media plays in spreading hate speech, harassment and incitement to violence,"[98] says Joan Donovan, director of the Technology and Social Change project at the Harvard Kennedy School's Shorenstein Center.

But as social media platforms grow, moderating content gets more difficult. Tech companies use artificial intelligence and algorithms to sort through the massive amounts of content they publish. But those tools sometimes have trouble determining what is offensive or unacceptable. It took years for YouTube to figure out how to remove white supremacist content while keeping historical content about Nazis and World War II. Deciding whether content is dehumanizing or bullying can also be difficult. Digital media expert Jessa Lingel says that language is not necessarily good or bad: "Context matters," she says. Because of this, social media platforms cannot rely on technology alone to effectively moderate content. "We need humans," says Lingel. "The tech just isn't there yet."[99]

The technology sector's crackdown on hate speech has also upset some conservatives, who argue that social media companies are unfairly targeting conservative voices. While some legal scholars argue that these private companies have the right to exclude what they want, some complain that it is nearly impossible to understand why a particular piece of content might be removed. Republican senator Ted Cruz says, "What makes the threat of political censorship so problematic is the lack of transparency, the invisibility, the ability for a handful of giant tech companies to decide if a particular speaker is disfavored."[100]

Tech companies admit that their employees are overwhelmingly liberal and that they have sometimes made mistakes in moderating content. But some believe that conservatives have offered no evidence of a systematic effort to censor right-leaning voices. Democratic senator Mazie Hirono says that Congress needs to increase oversight of tech companies regarding the rise of hate speech and disinformation but says that she dismisses the allegations of anticonservative bias, "which have been disproven time and time again."[101]

The Power of the Individual

While social media companies are taking stronger steps to ban hateful speech, individuals can also do more to limit the spread of extremist ideas. The internet gives users a power once reserved for journalists, but with that power comes responsibility. One way that users can be more responsible is to ask themselves a simple

Daryl Davis, pictured giving a presentation about race in America in 2019, is a black musician who has spent much of his time befriending members of the KKK and helping them leave the group.

question before they post or share: "Am I contributing something negative to my social network or something that can add context and understanding?"

Individuals can also make a conscious decision to engage more with people and points of view that are different from their own. This applies not just to the online world but to the "real" world as well. For example, Daryl Davis is a black musician who for the past thirty years has spent much of his time befriending members of the KKK. The seed was planted one night after a concert when a white man sat down beside Davis to talk about music and share a drink. The man admitted that he was a member of the KKK. Davis was struck by the fact that a black man and a KKK member could enjoy sitting together and talking. He says:

> When two enemies are talking, they're not fighting. It's when the talking ceases that the ground becomes fertile for violence. If you spend five minutes with your worst enemy . . . you will find that you both have something in common. As you build upon those commonalities, you're forming a relationship and as you build about that relationship, you're forming a friendship. That's what would happen. I didn't convert anybody. They saw the light and converted themselves.[102]

Davis says that once a friendship blossoms, Klan members begin to realize that maybe their hate is unjustified. Over the years, Davis has helped over two hundred Klan members give up their robes. When they do, he takes the robes and keeps them in his house as a reminder of how sitting down and talking with people can help prevent the spread of hate and extremism.

SOURCE NOTES

Introduction: A Growing Threat

1. Quoted in Simon Romero et al., "Walmart Store Connected Cultures, Until a Killer 'Came Here for Us,'" *New York Times*, August 4, 2019. www.nytimes.com.

2. Quoted in Christal Hayes et al., "Who Is Robert Bowers? Accused Pittsburgh Synagogue Shooter Left Anti-Semitic Trail," *USA Today*, October 27, 2018. www.usatoday.com.

3. Quoted in Liam Stack, "Over 1,000 Hate Groups Are Now Active in United States, Civil Rights Group Says," *New York Times*, February 20, 2019. www.nytimes.com.

4. Southern Poverty Law Center, "Frequently Asked Questions About Hate Groups," October 4, 2017. www.splcenter.org.

5. Quoted in Michael Biesecker et al., "El Paso Suspect Appears to Have Posted Anti-Immigrant Screed," Associated Press, August 4, 2019. www.apnews.com.

6. Quoted in Nicole Chavez et al., "Pittsburgh Synagogue Gunman Said He Wanted All Jews to Die, Criminal Complaint Says," CNN, October 31, 2018. www.cnn.com.

7. Quoted in Steve Miller, "Muslims and Government Officials Plan Next Steps in Christchurch," VOA News, March 19, 2019. www.voanews.com.

8. Quoted in Daniel L. Byman, "Terrorism and the Threat to Democracy," Brookings Institution, February 2019. www.brookings.edu.

Chapter One: The Changing Face of Hate

9. Quoted in Adam Gopnik, "Pour One Out for Ulysses S. Grant," *New Yorker*, September 25, 2017. www.newyorker.com.

10. Quoted in Allyson Hobbs, "A Hundred Years Later, 'The Birth of a Nation' Hasn't Gone Away," *New Yorker*, December 13, 2017. www.newyorker.com.

11. Heidi Beirich, "The Year in Hate: Rage Against Change," Southern Poverty Law Center, February 20, 2019. www.spl center.org.

12. Quoted in Noel King, "Jason Kessler on His 'Unite the Right' Rally Move to D.C.," NPR, August 10, 2018. www.npr.org.

13. Quoted in Emily Shugerman, "What White Supremacist Groups Look Like, 50 Years After Martin Luther King's Assassination," *The Independent* (London), April 3, 2018. www .independent.co.uk.

14. Quoted in Ray Sanchez, "Who Are White Nationalists and What Do They Want?," CNN, August 13, 2017. www.cnn.com.

15. Quoted in Sanchez, "Who Are White Nationalists and What Do They Want?"

16. Quoted in Peter Baker and Michael D. Shear, "El Paso Shooting Suspect's Manifesto Echoes Trump's Language," *New York Times*, August 4, 2019. www.nytimes.com.

17. Quoted in Lauretta Charleton, "What Is the Great Replacement?," *New York Times*, August 6, 2019. www.nytimes.com.

18. Quoted in Allie Conti, "Neo-Nazi to Troll Army: 'We Have to Be Sexy' at the Big Alt-Right Rally," *Vice*, August 9, 2017. www .vice.com.

19. Quoted in Sanchez, "Who Are White Nationalists and What Do They Want?"

20. Quoted in Sanchez, "Who Are White Nationalists and What Do They Want?"

21. Matthew N. Lyons, "Ctrl-Alt-Delete: The Origins and Ideology of the Alternative Right," Political Research Associates, January 20, 2017. www.politicalresearch.org.

22. Quoted in Ayesha Rascoe, "A Year After Charlottesville, Not Much Has Changed for Trump," NPR, August 11, 2018. www.npr.org.

23. Quoted in Dominique Mosbergen, "Neo-Nazi Site Daily Stormer Praises Trump's Charlottesville Reaction: 'He Loves Us All,'" HuffPost, August 13, 2017. www.huffpost.com.
24. Quoted in Mosbergen, "Neo-Nazi Site Daily Stormer Praises Trump's Charlottesville Reaction."
25. Quoted in William Cummings, "Former KKK Leader David Duke Praises Trump for His 'Courage,'" *USA Today*, August 15, 2017. www.usatoday.com.

Chapter Two: Ripe Conditions for Hate

26. Brian Levin, "Why White Supremacist Attacks Are on the Rise, Even in Surprising Places," *Time*, March 21, 2019. www.time.com.
27. Quoted in William McKenzie, "What Are We So Afraid of When It Comes to Immigration?," *Dallas Morning News*, January 23, 2018. www.dallasnews.com.
28. Quoted in Eduardo Porter and Karl Russell, "Migrants Are on the Rise Around the World, and Myths About Them Are Shaping Attitudes," *New York Times*, June 20, 2018. www.nytimes.com.
29. Quoted in Anti-Defamation League, "14 Words," 2020. www.adl.org.
30. Monica Duffy Toft, "White Right? How Demographics Is Changing US Politics," The Conversation, January 7, 2019. http://theconversation.com.
31. Quoted in Associated Press, "Supremacists Hope for Boost from Obama Win," NBC News, August 8, 2008. www.nbcnews.com.
32. Quoted in Patrik Jonsson, "After Obama's Win, White Backlash Festers in US," *Christian Science Monitor*, November 17, 2008. www.csmonitor.com.
33. Quoted in Jessica Reaves, "Mapping the Male Supremacy Movement: Women as Housekeepers with Wombs," *Ms.*, August 7, 2018. https://msmagazine.com.
34. Quoted in Stephanie Russell-Kraft, "The Rise of Male Supremacist Groups," *New Republic*, April 4, 2018. https://newrepublic.com.

35. Southern Poverty Law Center, "Male Supremacy." www.spl center.org.

36. Quoted in Steve Inskeep, "Hidden Brain: America's Changing Attitudes Toward Gay People," NPR, April 17, 2019. www .npr.org.

37. Quoted in Haeyoun Park and Iaryna Mykhyalyshyn, "L.G.B.T. People Are More Likely to Be Targets of Hate Crimes than Any Other Minority Group," *New York Times*, June 16, 2016. www.nytimes.com.

38. Quoted in Grace Hauck, "Anti-LGBT Hate Crimes Are Rising, the FBI Says. But It Gets Worse," *USA Today*, June 28, 2019. www.usatoday.com.

39. Quoted in Aaron M. Renn, "De-industrialization and the Displaced Worker," *Governing*, May 2016. www.governing.com.

40. Quoted in Mark Strauss, "Antiglobalism's Jewish Problem," YaleGlobal Online, November 12, 2003. https://yaleglobal .yale.edu.

41. Jamie Bartlett, "From Hope to Hate: How the Early Internet Fed the Far Right," *The Guardian* (Manchester), August 31, 2017. www.theguardian.com.

42. Quoted in Uri Friedman, "Trust Is Collapsing in America," *The Atlantic*, January 21, 2018. www.theatlantic.com.

43. Angela Nagle, "The Lost Boys," *The Atlantic*, December 2017. www.theatlantic.com.

Chapter Three: Spreading Hate Through the Internet

44. Quoted in Breanna Edwards, "Accused Charleston, SC, Shooter 'Self-Radicalized' Online, Prosecutors Say," The Root, August 23, 2016. www.theroot.com.

45. Quoted in Ben Collins, "Instagram Account Connected to Gilroy Shooter Pushed Staple of White Supremacist Internet Forums," NBC News, July 29, 2019. www.nbcnews.com.

46. Quoted in Ian Sample, "Tim Berners-Lee Launches Campaign to Save the Web from Abuse," *The Guardian* (Manchester), November 5, 2018. www.theguardian.com.

47. Quoted in Friedman, "Trust Is Collapsing in America."

48. Jennifer Szalai, "In 'Antisocial,' How the Alt-Right Went Viral," *New York Times*, October 7, 2019. www.nytimes.com.

49. Quoted in Jessica Guynn, "If You've Been Harassed Online, You're Not Alone. More than Half of Americans Say They've Experienced Hate," *USA Today*, February 13, 2019. www.usatoday.com.

50. Quoted in Matthew Shaer, "What Emotion Goes Viral the Fastest?," *Smithsonian*, April 2014. www.smithsonianmag.com.

51. Quoted in Robert Ruszkowski et al., "A Former White Supremacist's Warning: No One's Properly Addressing Online Extremism," NBC News, August 12, 2019. www.nbcnews.com.

52. Quoted in Katy Steinmetz, "How the Internet Can Make Hate Seem Normal—and Why That's So Dangerous," *Time*, October 31, 2018. https://time.com.

53. Vijaya Gadde and Del Harvey, "Creating New Policies Together," *Twitter Blog*, September 25, 2018. https://blog.twitter.com.

54. Quoted in Steinmetz, "How the Internet Can Make Hate Seem Normal—and Why That's So Dangerous."

55. Thompson, "Why the Internet Is So Polarized, Extreme, and Screamy."

56. Quoted in Douglas Van Praet, "Is the Internet Making Us Racist?," *Psychology Today*, December 15, 2015. www.psychologytoday.com.

57. Joan Donovan, "How Hate Groups' Secret Sound System Works," *The Atlantic*, March 17, 2019. www.theatlantic.com.

58. Quoted in Hanna Ingber, "The New Zealand Attack Posed New Challenges for Journalists. Here Are the Decisions the *Times* Made," *New York Times*, March 19, 2019. www.nytimes.com.

59. Quoted in Neil MacFarquhar, "Nazi Symbols and Racist Memes: Combating School Intolerance," *New York Times*, November 23, 2019. www.nytimes.com.

60. Quoted in MacFarquhar, "Nazi Symbols and Racist Memes."

61. Megan Condis, "From *Fortnite* to Alt-Right," *New York Times*, March 27, 2019. www.nytimes.com.

62. Quoted in Wes Enzinna, "Inside the Radical, Uncomfortable Movement to Reform White Supremacists," *Mother Jones*, July/August 2019. www.motherjones.com.

63. Quoted in MacFarquhar, "Nazi Symbols and Racist Memes."

Chapter Four: Leaving Hate and Extremism Behind

64. Quoted in Enzinna, "Inside the Radical, Uncomfortable Movement to Reform White Supremacists."

65. Quoted in Enzinna, "Inside the Radical, Uncomfortable Movement to Reform White Supremacists."

66. Life After Hate, "Who We Are," 2019. www.lifeafterhate.org.

67. Quoted in Josh Allen, "One-Time Skinhead Arno Michaels Helps Youths Respond with Compassion," *Christian Science Monitor*, August 3, 2012. www.csmonitor.com.

68. Quoted in Claire Bates, "I Was a Neo-Nazi. Then I Fell in Love with a Black Woman," BBC News, August 29, 2017. www.bbc.com.

69. Quoted in Bates, "I Was a Neo-Nazi. Then I Fell in Love with a Black Woman."

70. Quoted in Bates, "I Was a Neo-Nazi. Then I Fell in Love with a Black Woman."

71. Quoted in Jason Wilson, "Life After White Supremacy: The Former Neo-Fascist Now Working to Fight Hate," *The Guardian* (Manchester), April 4, 2017. www.theguardian.com.

72. Quoted in Enzinna, "Inside the Radical, Uncomfortable Movement to Reform White Supremacists."

73. Quoted in Enzinna, "Inside the Radical, Uncomfortable Movement to Reform White Supremacists."

74. Quoted in Yara Bayoumy and Kathy Gilsinan, "A Reformed White Nationalist Says the Worst Is Yet to Come," *The Atlantic*, August 6, 2019. www.theatlantic.com.

75. Quoted in Enzinna, "Inside the Radical, Uncomfortable Movement to Reform White Supremacists."

76. Quoted in Enzinna, "Inside the Radical, Uncomfortable Movement to Reform White Supremacists."

77. Quoted in Enzinna, "Inside the Radical, Uncomfortable Movement to Reform White Supremacists."

78. Quoted in Enzinna, "Inside the Radical, Uncomfortable Movement to Reform White Supremacists."

79. Quoted in Jessica Wacker, "Preview: 'The Anatomy of Hate: A Dialogue for Hope,'" Met Media, 2012. www.mymetmedia.com.

80. Quoted in Bates, "I Was a Neo-Nazi. Then I Fell in Love with a Black Woman."

81. Quoted in Enzinna, "Inside the Radical, Uncomfortable Movement to Reform White Supremacists."

82. Quoted in Bates, "I Was a Neo-Nazi. Then I Fell in Love with a Black Woman."

83. Quoted in Southern Poverty Law Center, "Why They Join," February 25, 2014. www.splcenter.org.

84. Quoted in Bates, "I Was a Neo-Nazi. Then I Fell in Love with a Black Woman."

85. Quoted in Allen, "One-Time Skinhead Arno Michaels Helps Youths Respond with Compassion."

86. Quoted in Allen, "One-Time Skinhead Arno Michaels Helps Youths Respond with Compassion."

Chapter Five: Responding to Hate and Extremism

87. Quoted in Southern Poverty Law Center, "Why They Join."

88. Quoted in Southern Poverty Law Center, "Why They Join."

89. Communities Against Hate, "About," 2020. https://communitiesagainsthate.org.

90. Quoted in Lexy Perez, "NBCUniversal Cable Entertainment Launches 'Erase the Hate' Campaign Anthem with Timbaland, Princess Nokia," *Hollywood Reporter*, September 9, 2018. www.hollywoodreporter.com.

91. Quoted in Human Rights First, "Islam Is Peace: Let's Remember George W. Bush's Words After 9/11," Human Rights First, February 2, 2017. www.humanrightsfirst.org.

92. Quoted in Clare Foran, "Donald Trump and the Rise of Anti-Muslim Violence," *The Atlantic*, September 22, 2016. www.theatlantic.com.

93. Quoted in Catherine Devine and Lilliana Byington, "Millions Are Victims of Hate Crimes, Though Many Never Report Them," Center for Public Integrity, August 16, 2018. https://publicintegrity.org.

94. Quoted in Devine and Byington, "Millions Are Victims of Hate Crimes, Though Many Never Report Them."

95. Quoted in Hannah Allam and Marisa Peñaloza, "'We Need to Evolve': Police Get Help to Improve Hate Crime Tracking," NPR, May 28, 2019. www.npr.org.

96. Quoted in MacFarquhar, "Nazi Symbols and Racist Memes."

97. Quoted in MacFarquhar, "Nazi Symbols and Racist Memes."

98. Quoted in Audie Cornish, "Big Tech Companies Are Struggling with How to Best Police Their Platforms," NPR, July 11, 2019. www.npr.org.

99. Quoted in Sara Harrison, "Twitter and Instagram Unveil New Ways to Combat Hate—Again," *Wired*, July 11, 2019. www.wired.com.

100. Quoted in Jessica Guynn, "Ted Cruz Threatens to Regulate Facebook, Google and Twitter over Charges of Anti-Conservative Bias," *USA Today*, April 10, 2019. www.usatoday.com.

101. Quoted in Guynn, "Ted Cruz Threatens to Regulate Facebook, Google and Twitter over Charges of Anti-Conservative Bias."

102. Quoted in Dwane Brown, "How One Man Convinced 200 Ku Klux Klan Members to Give Up Their Robes," NPR, August 20, 2017. www.npr.org.

ORGANIZATIONS AND WEBSITES

Anti-Defamation League (ADL) — www.adl.org

The ADL offers a large variety of anti-hate programs and resources. The Research and Tools section on its website includes a Hate Symbols Database that provides a list of symbols used by white supremacist groups and other types of hate groups.

Center for the Study of Hate and Extremism
https://csbs.csusb.edu/hate-and-extremism-center

A nonpartisan research and policy center, the Center for the Study of Hate and Extremism provides objective information regarding hate and bias to government officials, law enforcement, scholars, community activists, the media, and others.

Federal Bureau of Investigation (FBI) — www.fbi.gov

The FBI investigates and seeks to prevent crimes based on bias against race, religion, ethnicity, sexual orientation, or gender identity. By entering the phrase "hate crimes" into the FBI website search engine, visitors can find the FBI's year-by-year statistics on the number of hate crimes that are committed in the United States.

Life After Hate — www.lifeafterhate.org

This organization, founded by former members of the white power movement, is committed to helping people exit hate groups and supporting those who have already left. Life After Hate uses a variety of strategies such as education, public awareness campaigns, and job training programs to help individuals reenter society and make positive contributions.

Serve 2 Unite—www.giftofourwounds.com/serve2unite

Serve 2 Unite is an organization dedicated to providing students with a healthy sense of purpose, belonging, and identity in order to steer them away from hateful, violent ideologies, bullying, gun violence, substance abuse, school shootings, and other negative pursuits.

Southern Poverty Law Center (SPLC)—www.splcenter.org

The SPLC monitors hate groups in America, reporting on their activities and rhetoric. The organization has made a number of its reports available on its website, including Extremist Files, which lists the most prominent hate groups in the United States, and a hate map, which shows city-by-city locations of more than one thousand American hate groups.

FOR FURTHER RESEARCH

Books

Andrew Marantz, *Antisocial: Online Extremists, Techno-Utopians, and the Hijacking of the American Conversation*. New York: Viking, 2019.

Angela Nagle, *Kill All Normies*. Croydon, UK: Zero, 2017.

David Neiwert, *Alt-America: The Rise of the Radical Right in the Age of Trump*. New York: Verso, 2017.

Christian Picciolini, *Breaking Hate: Confronting the New Culture of Extremism*. New York: Hachette, 2020.

Alexandra Minna Stern, *Proud Boys and the White Ethnostate: How the Alt-Right Is Warping the American Imagination*. Boston: Beacon, 2019.

Internet Sources

Joseph Cox and Jason Koebler, "Why Won't Twitter Treat White Supremacy like ISIS? Because It Would Mean Banning Some Republican Politicians Too," *Vice*, April 25, 2019. www.vice.com.

Sean Illing, "This Filmmaker Spent Months Interviewing Neo-Nazis and Jihadists. Here's What She Learned," *Vox*, March 17, 2019. www.vox.com.

Sharon Jayson and Kaiser Health News, "What Makes People Join Hate Groups?," *U.S. News & World Report*, August 23, 2017. www.usnews.com.

Clarence Page, "How White Supremacy Morphed into White 'Victimization,'" *Lafayette (LA) Daily Advertiser*, August 17, 2017. www.theadvertiser.com.

Southern Poverty Law Center, "Ten Ways to Fight Hate," August 14, 2017. www.splcenter.org.

Websites

ProPublica (https://projects.propublica.org). A New York–based organization that pursues investigative journalism, ProPublica spent a year documenting hate crime. The website's Documenting Hate project includes numerous stories written by ProPublica journalists. Victims of hate crimes or others who witnessed hate crimes are invited to submit their stories to the project.

Stories About Hate Crimes, NPR (www.npr.org/tags/131511550 /hate-crimes). NPR has assembled many stories about hate crimes, including coverage of the nine murders in Charleston, South Carolina, committed by Dylann Roof. Visitors can read transcripts of NPR stories on hate crimes and also listen to the broadcasts, which are archived on the site.

INDEX